PIPPA
AND THE
MAJOR

Written by
Adam Fisk and Fia Perera

Illustrations by
Vu Danh

Lettering by
Leigh Walls

Additional artwork by
Ben Fisk

Special Thanks
Sheila FitzGerald & Arpad Voros -
The Old Yarmouth Inn

2022
FISKY
ENTERPRISES

William James Thacher was born in 1736 to a wealthy British industrialist, Thomas Thacher, and his wife, Mary. He's the youngest of 3 brothers. His two older brothers Charles and Montague are leadership material and eventually enter the military and get married into society.

William is a sensitive soul. As a child, he loves to spend time in the country with his best friend Sebastian Hornsby, who he nicknames Bash. William is passionate about painting and the arts even putting on plays with the servant children, much to his parent's chagrin.

Unlike his brothers, William has no real aspirations to join the army. He's close to his mother Mary, a strong, athletic, commanding woman who excels at archery and fencing. Mary never had a daughter and loves William's passion for the arts and his sensitivity which she encourages.

Thomas is increasingly concerned about his son.

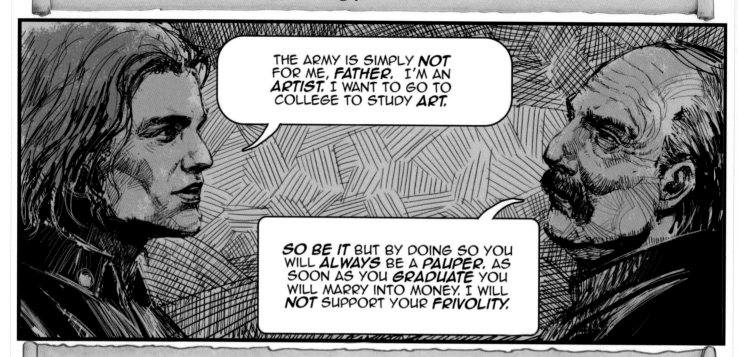

Mary gets busy matchmaking and introduces William to Daphne Snodgrass Smythe – 7th cousin to the Queen and an only child who will become the Duchess of Dartford. Daphne has always been smitten with William who doesn't feel the same way.

As he is an excellent scholar and artist, William is accepted into Oxford University. Being a gifted sportsman, Bash is also accepted. Very soon the pair are stalwarts of the party circuit.

Bash's party piece de resistance is to dress up as a hideous old Duchess of Dandruff – always poking fun at Daphne.

Their wild behavior almost gets them expelled from the prestigious college several times.

NEXT TIME YOU ARE BOTH *OUT!*

But the threats never come to fruition due to the boys redeeming themselves as a result of William's artistry and Bash's sporting achievements.

The Reverend, despite being very austere has a huge, secret, soft spot for his wild, untamed daughter who often embarrasses him with her unladylike pursuits of horseback riding and championing Native American and Animal Rights.

But Pippa's actions get more and more serious. She decides to target the rich ladies who have gathered for Yarmouth's prestigious annual fur fashion show which has been organized by Pippa's arch-enemy and the Mayor's daughter, Felicity Bunkle, the main model on the primitive raised wooden catwalk. However, as she sets down the runway Pippa gives the signal to several Native American boys with ropes who pull the catwalk apart catapulting Felicity into a 3-foot-deep pit of cow shit.

This pitches Pippa into real trouble.

Her father has to pay for all the damages and is nearly ruined.

Mayor Bunkle pushes for jail time but Pippa's father dissuades him by agreeing to marry Pippa off to his evil, unpopular son Felix, who his father fears will never find a wife.

However, Pippa's family is still in ruin and is now having to sell their house and the church. Pippa's mother is despondent and her father is not speaking to her.

I HATE THAT *IDIOT* MAYOR *BUNKLE* AND HIS *DISGUSTING* OFFSPRING.

THERE IS TALK IN THE TRIBE THAT HE HAS *EYES* ON OUR *RESERVATION.* HE IS MAKING GIFTS OF *TOBACCO* AND *ALCOHOL* TO THE ELDERS IN *EXCHANGE* FOR SMALL PARCELS OF OUR *LAND* AND I FEAR THE WORST AS THEY ARE *NAÏVE* TO HIS *TRICKERY.*

Pippa's Uncle Louis comes to her with an idea to save her family from further ruin.

He convinces Pippa that she can win the next big horse race in Boston with her 18-hand stallion, Black Sky but no one must know it is her competing or that she's a woman, which is banned.

Meanwhile, William who has only been in the New World for 2 weeks learns that he is to be stationed at Yarmouth Port after his officer training in Boston. Life in the barracks is unbelievably dull so he and Bash decide to enter an all-comers horse race along with other officers who want to send a message that the British are infinitely better horsemen than the settlers.

The next morning the 40 or so riders and horses exit the paddock area and approach the track which effectively is just two channels cut through the trees. The starter explains that they will race up the first channel, turn at the top, race down the second channel and the winner will be the first to break a red ribbon at the finish line.

William is amazed at the sheer disorganization. Drunken people are everywhere. The crowd buzzes with last-minute betting, arguments, and screams of support.

Many of the horses are spooked by all the noise. William fights to calm his horse down while threats and taunts are traded between the British riders, many of whom are cavalry officers, and the local Americans.

I *SAY*, CAN'T YOU SIMPLY *BUGGER OFF* YOU UPPER-CLASS, *NITWIT!*

As William is jostling to get close to the start line one horse and rider, in particular, catches his attention. Hanging back from the melee is a magnificent, huge black horse with a slightly built rider in a black outfit, riding bareback with a hood covering his face.

The race starts with the loud bang of a musket shot which is a surprise to more than one of the riders. Several of them are left in the mud as their horses spook, rear up, throw off their riders and gallop off.

BAAANG!!!!

William and Bash are in the middle of the pack fending off the competitors attempting to push them into the trees as local children hurl stones at them. At the halfway point only a handful of the horses still have riders and as they turn in the sludge. It's almost impossible to dodge the riderless horses sliding around and crashing into each other. It's complete mayhem.

After the corner, the gallop to the finish line commences and William, closely followed by Bash leads in front.

With only 100 yards left to go a horse and rider suddenly fly past them.

Though his vision is blurred, William catches a glimpse of the bareback rider nimbly perched on the horse. As their coattails rise he sees the shape of what appears to be a fabulous, very feminine behind.

By the time they reach the finish line the stallion is already many lengths ahead. William and Bash pick up second and third but all the prize money goes to the mysterious rider. A few minutes later they enter the winner's circle to a cacophony of cheering and screaming. The slight rider holds up the winning purse flanked protectively by the colorful Native American and an elderly man who makes a short speech congratulating his nephew, "Philip" who stands quietly now wearing a gentleman's wig as the crowd applauds. William turns to Bash noticing that he and the Native American are intensely gazing at each other smiling.

William laughs as the two are led to the podium to accept their runner-up awards. Bash makes a beeline to Sparkle.

WHAT A *STYLISH* OUTFIT. I *LOVE* YOUR USE OF *COLOR*. WHAT IS THIS *TEXTURE?*

IT'S AN ANGORA AND COTTON BLEND AND WOULD LOOK EVEN *BETTER* IF I HAD *BEAUTIFUL* BLUE EYES LIKE *YOURS*.

NOW YOU ARE NO LONGER A *PALEFACE*. YOUR RED *CHEEKS* MATCH YOUR *UNIFORM*.

*M*eanwhile, William walks up to congratulate "Philip" but Uncle Louis blocks his way with a protective look. Trying not to gape, he notices that the young man is very feminine in looks and that his beard is no longer evenly spaced on his face but is now slightly askew.

As he attempts to engage with Philip, a large commotion starts. A man approaches the podium stating that the race was not fairly won and that the winning rider was too light as he didn't have a saddle. All hell breaks loose and William and Bash have to defend themselves against the mad, drunk crowd. Order is restored as the organizers announce that this was a free for all race with no weight restrictions. With order restored, William turns to where the winners were standing but they have disappeared into the early evening hue.

THIS IS SO *ITCHY*. I DON'T KNOW *HOW* YOU MEN *STAND* IT. IT'S LIKE HAVING *PUBIC HAIR* ON MY *FACE!*

IT *IS* PUBIC HAIR.

THE *WHOLE* TRIBE CONTRIBUTED. WE ARE *NOT* HAIRY PEOPLE.

Pippa gives her Father all the money which he grudgingly accepts, even though it was from a legitimate horse race. People are compensated for their losses. However, trouble is brewing as Bunkle is still intent on the marriage going ahead. Reverend Longbottom is disgusted at the thought of Felix marrying his beloved Pippa and fights against it but Bunkle threatens to close the church if the wedding does not go ahead in one month and the Reverend has to concede. You have to understand that Otto Bunkle was a force to be reckoned with. He was manipulative, mean, and well connected and people were afraid of him. He had ingratiated himself with the British military hierarchy in Boston as he wanted the British favor to further his political career. He was not a man to be crossed or trusted.

Pippa is devastated and that night she and Sparkle weigh up their options.

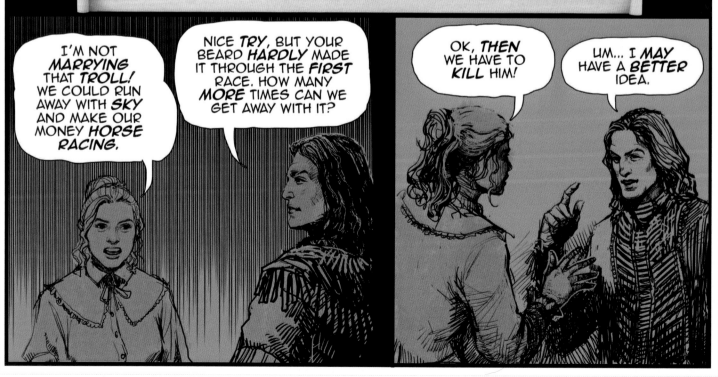

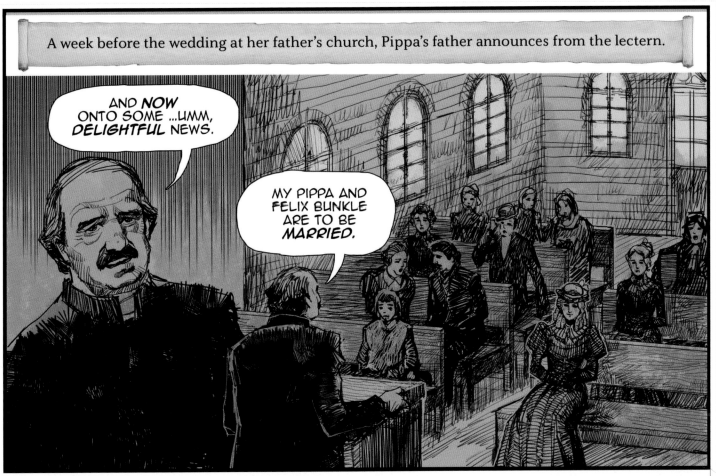

Watching this strange event unfold from the corner of the church with raised eyebrows are two young British officers who have just been stationed at the Yarmouth militia. After the service, they are to be introduced to the congregation.

MAY *GOD* BE *WITH* THAT YOUNG MAN... MOVING ON. *ONE* MORE ORDER OF *BUSINESS.* I HAVE BEEN ASKED BY GENERAL PRESTON PIMPLE TO INTRODUCE TWO *FINE YOUNG* BRITISH OFFICERS WHO WILL BE IN CHARGE OF THE MILITIA *PROTECTING* OUR PORT.

CAPTAIN WILLIAM THACHER AND LIEUTENANT SEBASTIAN HORNSBY

I *KNOW* THEM. THEY'RE FROM THE *RACE.* DO YOU THINK THEY'LL *RECOGNIZE* ME?

WITH THAT *BEARD,* NOT A *CHANCE.*

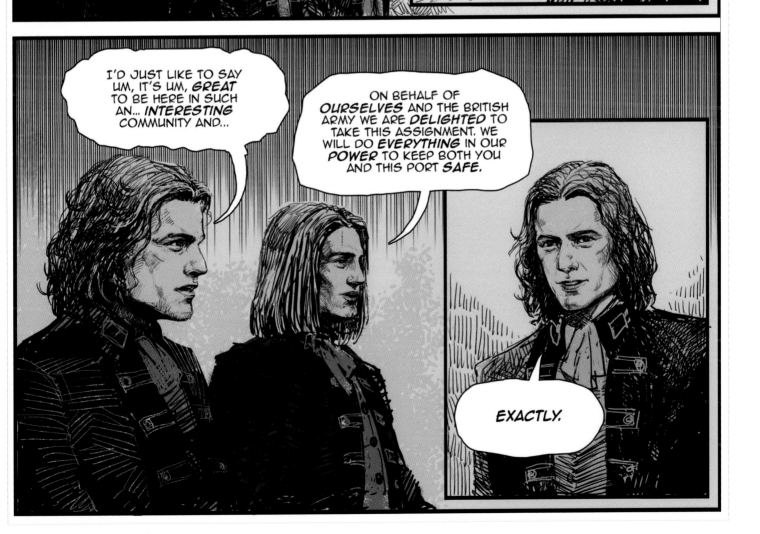

I'D JUST LIKE TO SAY UM, IT'S UM, *GREAT* TO BE HERE IN SUCH AN... *INTERESTING* COMMUNITY AND...

ON BEHALF OF *OURSELVES* AND THE BRITISH ARMY WE ARE *DELIGHTED* TO TAKE THIS ASSIGNMENT. WE WILL DO *EVERYTHING* IN OUR *POWER* TO KEEP BOTH YOU AND THIS PORT *SAFE.*

EXACTLY.

The next day at the town square a large gathering of disgruntled townspeople listen to the visiting tax collector who is joined on the stage by the Mayor. He informs them of their new and increased taxes. William and Bash who have been sequestered to keep the peace, stand next to Bunkle. They watch on uncomfortably.

WE CAN'T AFFORD THIS, YOU ARE *BLEEDING* US *DRY!*

DO YOUR JOB, *SIRS,* I WILL *NOT* HAVE THIS *MEETING* TURN INTO A *RABBLE.*

The next day William and Bash are standing at the Yarmouth Port dock close to the British garrison. They look on at the horrific scene as one whaling ship after another brings home their bloody loads. The sea is red.

Two of the Mayor's burly henchmen are scurrying around the scene and from the conversations the boys soon learn that they are collecting payments from the ship captains. One captain seems particularly agitated at the amount of money he has to hand over. Later, William approaches him in the tavern.

EXCUSE ME, SIR, *WHY* DID YOU *PAY* THESE MEN?

OH, THAT'S JUST THE *WAY* IT IS, *SIR*. THE MAYOR *CONTROLS* THIS PORT.

WELL *TECHNICALLY* THIS IS *CROWN LAND* AND *I* AM IN *COMMAND* OF THE PORT.

OH WELL SIR, *YOU'D* BEST TAKE THAT UP WITH THE *MAYOR* AND THE *GENERAL*. THEY'RE IN IT *TOGETHER* AND THERE'S *NOTHING* WE CAN DO ABOUT IT.

MY *DEAR* CAPTAIN, AS YOU MAY KNOW, I HAVE AN *EXCELLENT* RELATIONSHIP WITH GENERAL PIMPLE. WE HAVE ... SEVERAL *BUSINESS* ARRANGEMENTS THAT WE SHARE.

I WISH TO MAKE YOU *AWARE* THAT ALTHOUGH THE PORT IS OWNED *RESPECTFULLY* BY THE *CROWN* THE DAY-TO-DAY DEALINGS CONCERNING THE *WHALING* AND OTHER *MERCHANTS* ARE *MY* RESPONSIBILITY. IN KEEPING WITH THIS AGREEMENT, I WILL *REWARD* YOU WITH A FAIR COMMISSION.

YOU WISH TO *BUY* ME OFF SIR FOR TURNING A *BLIND EYE?*

YOU'RE A *SMART* YOUNG MAN AND IF I WERE YOU I WOULD NOT *DISOBEY* YOUR GENERAL.

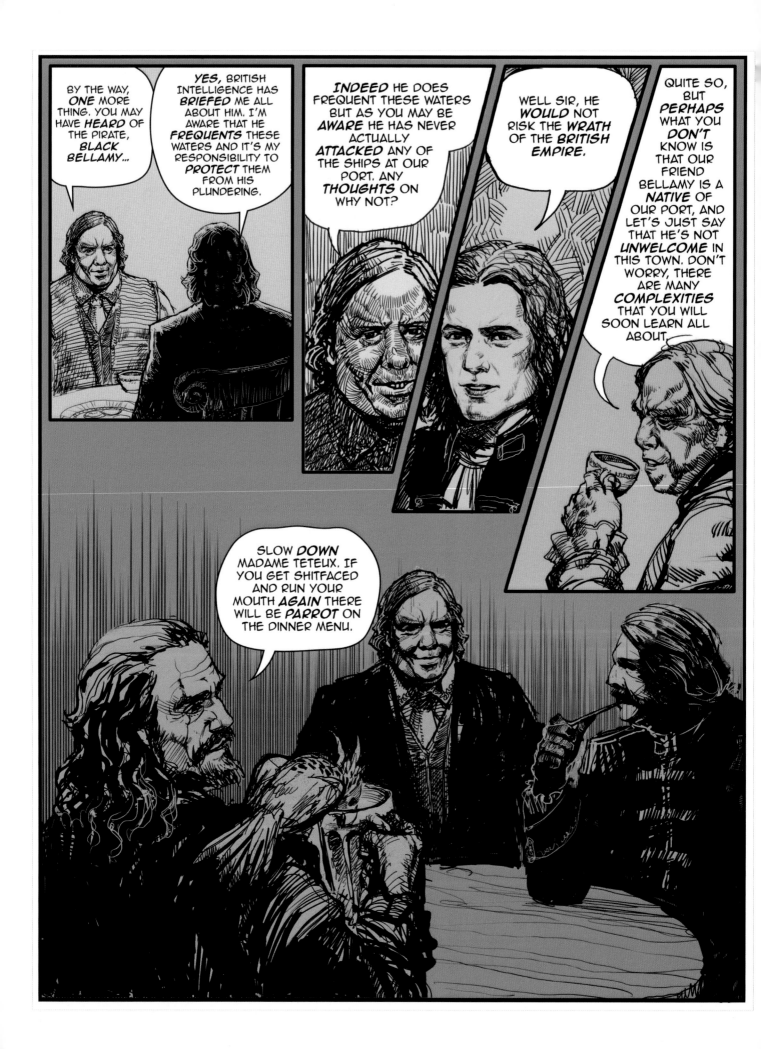

HONESTLY BASH, THIS GETS WORSE AND *WORSE*. BUNKLE IS GOING TO BE HARD TO HANDLE AND HE'S *RIGHT IN* WITH PIMPLE. HE'S A *GREEDY,* AMBITIOUS, LITTLE *SHIT* AND I SUSPECT THAT THE *NONSENSE* HE'S INVOLVED IN THE PORT IS JUST THE TIP OF THE *ICEBERG.* DO YOU KNOW I *SUSPECT* THAT HE'S WORKING WITH THAT BLOODY *PIRATE BELLAMY.* ON TOP OF *THAT,* I'D NO IDEA THAT THE *RELATIONS* WITH THE LOCAL COLONIALS ARE SO *BAD.* THEY DON'T *LIKE* US.

INDEED AND WORD IS THAT THINGS ARE HEATING UP WITH THE FRENCH IN *CANADA.* I HEAR THAT WE MAY BE *ASKED* TO JOIN SOME SORT OF *INVASION* FORCE SOON.

NOT *EXACTLY* TEA IN THE PARK IS IT?

OH I *DON'T* KNOW. BETTER THAN MARRYING OLD *DANDRUFF* AND ROTTING AWAY ON HER *SMELLY* FARM IN DARTMOUTH.

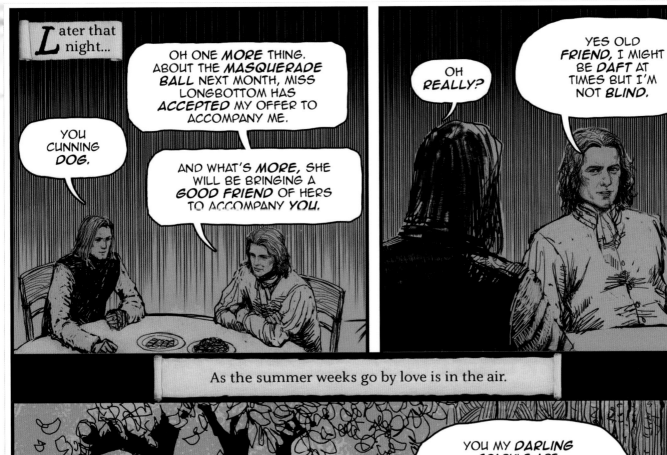

As the summer weeks go by love is in the air.

The Bunkles wasted no time. They got the elders drunk and had them trade their land for a pittance. The next day, William and Bash watch forlornly as Sparkle's tribe is cleared off the land by the British soldiers.

IT IS **NOT** THEIR FAULT. MY FATHER HAS BEEN **DECEIVED** BY THE BUNKLE'S **FIRE WATER** AND **TOBACCO.** HE TRADED ALL OUR **LAND** AND NOW WE MUST **GO.**

WILLIAM, DO **SOMETHING.** YOU KNOW THIS IS **WRONG!**

NOT NOW, **M'LADY.** THIS IS A WRONG THAT WILL BE **RIGHTED,** BUT FOR NOW WE MUST **PLAY** ALONG WITH THEIR **GAMES.**

In the coming weeks, Pippa spends much of her time with Sparkle and the tribe who have relocated to the marshland.

She teaches them to keep beehives and soon their artisanal honey becomes famous in the Boston area. She works with them to grow herbs, potatoes, and other vegetables in the rich marshland soil and their businesses start to flourish much to Felix and the Mayor's chagrin.

On top of the despicable treatment of the tribe Bunkle has upped his demand for whale blubber and now every day the slaughter of the whales gets worse.

WILLIAM, WE *MUST* PUT A *STOP* TO THIS SENSELESS *SLAUGHTER.*

I *KNOW,* MY DARLING, BUT RIGHT NOW MY *HANDS* ARE *TIED.* I KNOW THE OWNERS OF THESE SHIPS. BUNKLE CHARGES THEM A *FORTUNE* FOR USING THE DOCK AND GIVES THEM THE *LOWEST* PRICES FOR THE BLUBBER. I'M *SURE* THESE POOR BASTARDS WOULD DO *ANYTHING* TO GET OUT OF THIS *BLOODY* BUSINESS BUT THEY LIVE FROM HAND TO MOUTH — AS INDEED *ALL* THE LOCAL FISHERMEN. IF ONLY I HAD *ACCESS* TO MY FAMILY'S *MONEY,* I WOULD BUY THEM *OUT.*

AND DO *WHAT?*

TOURISM, BOSTONIANS COME HERE WEEK AFTER WEEK IN *DROVES* FOR FRESH AIR, THE *FINEST* CLAM CHOWDER, AND TO STROLL THE *BEACHES.* IMAGINE IF WE COULD TAKE THEM *OUT* TO SEE THESE *MAGNIFICENT* CREATURES. I *KNOW* *MOBY* WOULD PUT ON *QUITE* A SHOW FOR THEM.

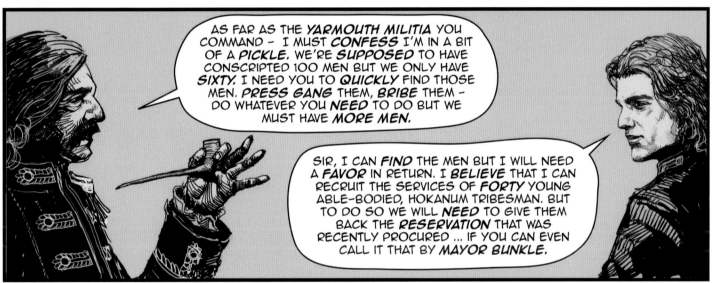

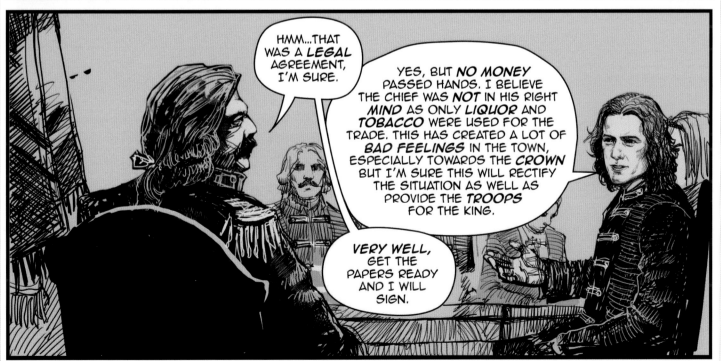

The next day William meets with Daphne while Bash supervises the return of the tribe to their land.

DAPH, THIS IS *HARD* FOR ME TO SAY AS YOU CAME *ALL* THIS WAY, BUT I'M NOT IN *LOVE* WITH YOU. THIS WHOLE *WEDDING BUSINESS* IS OUR PARENTS' DOING AND IF *TRUTH* BE TOLD, I'M IN LOVE WITH *SOMEONE ELSE.*

OH MY *GOD,* IS IT *BASH?*

OH *GOD* NO! BUT I THINK AT ONE POINT HE WOULD HAVE *LOVED* THAT.

HONESTLY WILLIAM, NO HARD *FEELINGS.* I WAS GOING SIMPLY *STIR CRAZY* IN DARTFORD, ANYWAY.

YOU KNOW I CAN'T *STAND* ALL THAT *SOCIETY NONSENSE* AND ENGLAND IS SUCH A *CRASHING* BORE THESE DAYS. I WAS GLAD TO HAVE AN *EXCUSE* TO GET AWAY.

THANK YOU, *DAPH.* ALL THIS HAS BEEN SUCH A *WEIGHT* ON MY SHOULDERS--

-- BUT BEFORE YOU LEAVE YOU *MUST* ATTEND THE *BUNKLE BALL.* I HEAR THEY ARE DELAYING IT UNTIL OUR RETURN FROM *CANADA.*

THEN I *WILL.*

NOW, YOU MAKE SURE YOU COME BACK *SAFELY. BOTH* OF YOU ARE *VERY* DEAR TO ME.

IF IT'S FROM THAT *CAD* WILLIAM, I *DON'T* WANT TO *READ* IT.

IT'S FROM WILLIAM. I *SUGGEST* YOU READ IT. HE CAN'T BE HERE *HIMSELF* AS HE'S *SUPERVISING* THE LOADING OF THE SHIP.

WE *LEAVE* IN 30 MINUTES. I MUST NOW HURRY THERE *MYSELF* WITH THESE *BRAVE* VOLUNTEERS.

*P*ippa angrily shoves the letter in her pocket as Bash gallops away. She turns her attention back to the local women erecting wigwams and gathering water. Later on curious as to what's in the letter she sits down and reads it.

HE'S ALL *YOURS*, PIPPA. OUR PROPOSED *ENGAGEMENT* IS *OVER*. HE LOVES *YOU*. I *HOPE* WE CAN BE... *FRIENDS*.

OH, AND *BEFORE* HE LEFT SPARKLE SAID THAT I *MUST* TELL YOU TO CHECK *"SKY'S"* STALL AS THERE IS A *SURPRISE* FOR *YOU*.

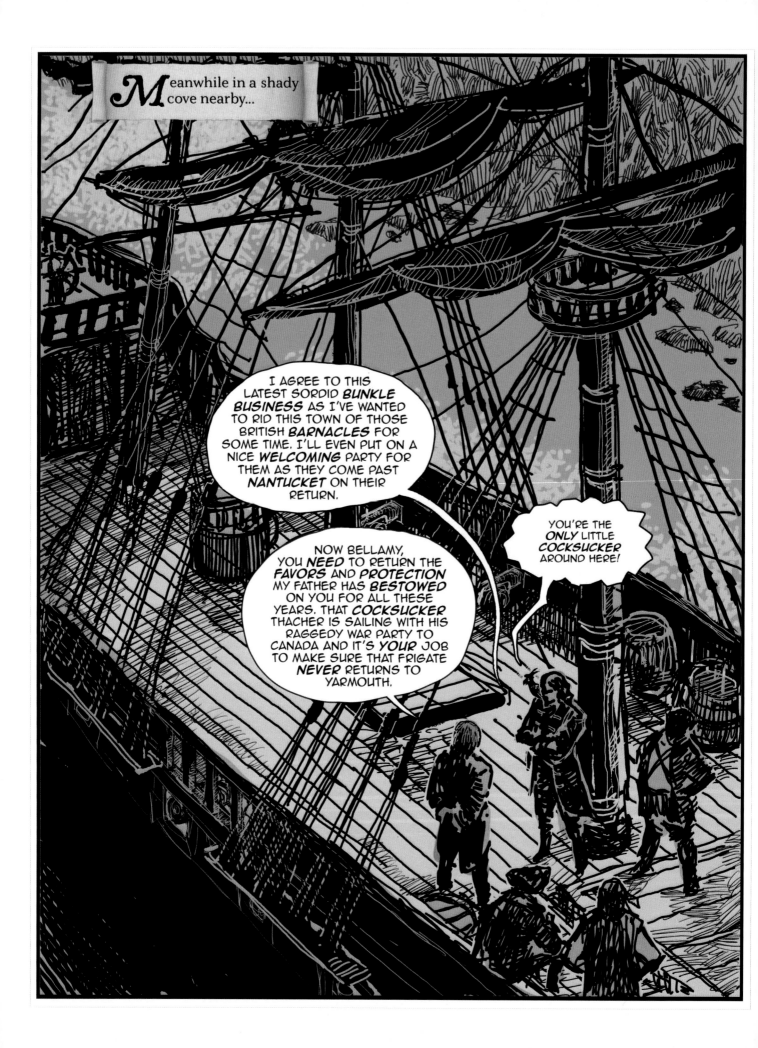

BUT HERE'S MORE *BUSINESS*. A *CHEST* OF MY *GOLD* HAS BEEN *STOLEN* FROM WHERE I HID IT AND I NEED IT *BACK*.

AND *YOU* ARE GOING TO *FIND* MY *GOLD* OR--

-- *YOU* WILL END UP LIKE THESE *BLAGGARDS*.

SEARED *BLAGGARD* BALLS WITH A PINCH OF *GARLIC*. *PARFAIT!*

On the evening of September 12th, 1759 the Yarmouth Port Frigate sailed up to the mouth of the St. Lawrence River near Quebec and moored close to the ship of the British Vice Admiral Charles Saunders. The British military commander General James Wolfe was waiting for them.

CAPTAIN THACHER AND LIEUTENANT HORNSBY I HAVE A *JOB* FOR YOU. WE NEED TO TAKE *QUEBEC*. OUR *ORIGINAL* PLAN WAS A FULL-FRONTAL ASSAULT *HERE--*

-- BUT THE *FROGS* ARE FAIRLY WELL DUG IN AND I DON'T HAVE THE *MANPOWER*. AFTER *THREE MONTHS* OF TRADING NOT SO MUCH AS *INSULTS* WITH EACH OTHER, THE TIME HAS COME FOR *ACTION*.

WE'VE BEEN *BEATING* UP THEIR SUPPLY LINES AND HAVE *ROUGHED* UP THE LOCALS BUT I CAN'T GET MONTCALM TO LEAVE HIS *FORT*. WINTER'S COMING AND I THINK THEY HAVE ENOUGH TO LAST OUT. THEY HAVE MORE *SUPPLIES* THAN US FOR SURE.

I HAVE AN IDEA TO *BREAK* THE *DEADLOCK* BUT IT'S FRANKLY GOING TO TAKE A LOT OF *GUTS*. I HEAR YOU COULD BE MY *MAN*.

YOU WILL *REPORT* TO COLONEL HOWE *HERE.*

L'Anse-au-Foulon

WELCOME *ABOARD,* THACHER.

HOWE IS GOING TO LEAD YOUR LOT AND 2 OTHER *COMPANIES* UP A CLIFF CALLED *L'ANSE-AU-FOULON.* ONCE WE ARE THERE THIS WILL GIVE US *DIRECT ACCESS* TO THE PLAINS OF ABRAHAM ABOVE FROM WHICH WE CAN *STRIKE* WITHOUT HAVING TO WORRY ABOUT THEIR DAMN *GUNS,* ARE YOU FOLLOWING?

PERFECTLY, SIR.

LISTEN, THACHER, I'VE HAD GOOD *REPORTS* ABOUT YOU AND I KNOW YOUR *BROTHERS* WELL SO I KNOW YOU'RE FROM *GOOD STOCK* BUT I'VE HEARD SOME ... *CONCERNS* ABOUT YOUR MAN HORNSBY. IS HE UP TO THE *JOB?*

HE IS, SIR. I WOULD STAKE MY *LIFE* ON IT.

LET'S *HOPE* YOU DON'T *HAVE* TO. WHAT ABOUT YOUR *INDIANS?* THEY LOOK A BIT *RAGTAG* TO ME.

THEY ARE *GOOD* AND *TRUE,* SIR.

GOOD, THEY *BETTER* BE GOOD *CLIMBERS.* I DON'T WANT TO MAKE A *MESS* OF THE BEACH. THERE'S NOT MUCH LEFT AFTER YOU FALL *150 FEET,* I DARE SAY – *DISMISSED.*

The climb didn't go well. The initial group of around 20 British light infantrymen resplendent in their red uniforms under the moonlight tried the climb but soon got stuck. A few got close but tragically lost their footing and fell. As soon as they hit the ground, men surrounded them to tend to their wounds and mute their screams. The first wave having failed, Howe briefs another group of men as William approaches. Howe barks orders at the visibly terrified Captain in charge of the next group of men to attempt the perilous climb.

EXCUSE MY INTERRUPTION, SIR, BUT THE *NATIVES* UNDER MY COMMAND ARE EXCELLENT *CLIMBERS* AND ARE DEAD KEEN ON SHOWING THEIR *MUSTER.* MAY WE GO *NEXT?*

DO YOU THINK FOR *ONE MINUTE* I WOULD RISK THE ENTIRE *SUCCESS* OF THIS MISSION ON YOU AND YOUR *RABBLE?*

INDEED, SIR--

-- WHAT WOULD YOU HAVE TO *LOSE?*

VERY WELL, *THACHER,* I WILL GIVE YOU A *CHANCE* BUT ANY NOISE AND I'LL HAVE THE LOT OF THEM *SHOT.* SO, FOR CHRIST'S SAKE CLIMB FAST AND *DIE QUIETLY.*

A few seconds later...

*O*nce all the men had reached the top they quickly found tree stumps nearby to tie ropes to before throwing them down to the redcoats waiting way below, but there was trouble ahead. Suddenly, agitated French voices were audible in the night and a shot rang out. A musket ball hit the ground near William forcing all the men to throw themselves down for cover.

WE NEED TO *SILENCE* THOSE *MUSKETS*. WE'RE SITTING *DUCKS*.

I'M ON *IT*.

The skirmish at the top of the cliff does not last long. The handful of French guarding the point is rounded up and taken prisoner. Bash and Sparkle had run clean through their lines and when the defenders had seen their bravery and intent they had thrown their muskets down and surrendered. Soon after hundreds of redcoats joined the men at the top of the cliff, ready to press their advantage.

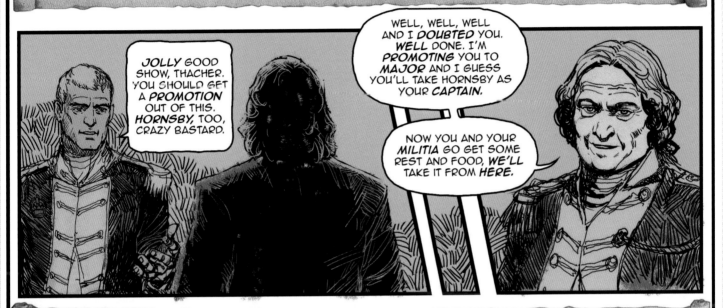

JOLLY GOOD SHOW, THACHER. YOU SHOULD GET A *PROMOTION* OUT OF THIS. *HORNSBY*, TOO, CRAZY BASTARD.

WELL, WELL, WELL AND I *DOUBTED* YOU. *WELL* DONE. I'M *PROMOTING* YOU TO *MAJOR* AND I GUESS YOU'LL TAKE HORNSBY AS YOUR *CAPTAIN.*

NOW YOU AND YOUR *MILITIA* GO GET SOME REST AND FOOD, *WE'LL* TAKE IT FROM *HERE.*

That was the last time the boys saw General Wolfe alive. Later that day the British overwhelmed the French and took Quebec but both Wolfe and the French Commander Montcalm were killed.

The boys stayed several days in the City but were eventually told to take their frigate back to Yarmouth and await orders. The tale of their bravery had spread and they and their Hokanum were treated as celebrities by the other troops. They couldn't have felt any happier as they took their boats back to the waiting frigate.

CONGRATULATIONS *CAPTAIN* AND WHILE I AM AT IT, WHAT THE *HELL* CAME OVER YOU UP THERE ON THE *RIDGE?*

I THOUGHT OF MY *FATHER* RANTING AWAY AT HOW I WOULD *NEVER* AMOUNT TO *ANYTHING* AND I *JUMPED* UP AND RAN. PERHAPS THERE'S A BIT OF *BRAWN* UNDER ALL MY *BEAUTY.*

All this time Pippa had been beside herself with worry. After the Frigate was out of sight she and Daphne went to the barn as Sparkle had instructed, only to find a fortune in Spanish doubloons in bags hidden deep in the hay. The next day they went to the Port and one by one did deals with each whaling Captain to procure their ships to be part of her eco-tourist fleet. No more whales would be killed on Pippa's watch.

NOW YOU ALL *WORK* FOR *ME*. I CAN'T *WAIT* TO SEE BUNKLE'S *FACE*.

NO *NEWS* YET, DAPHNE. I'M SO *WORRIED* AND IT'S *HELL* JUST SITTING HERE *WAITING*.

THEN LET'S NOT *WAIT*. YOU HAVE *SHIPS*. LET'S *SAIL* UP THE COAST AND FIND OUT FOR *OURSELVES*.

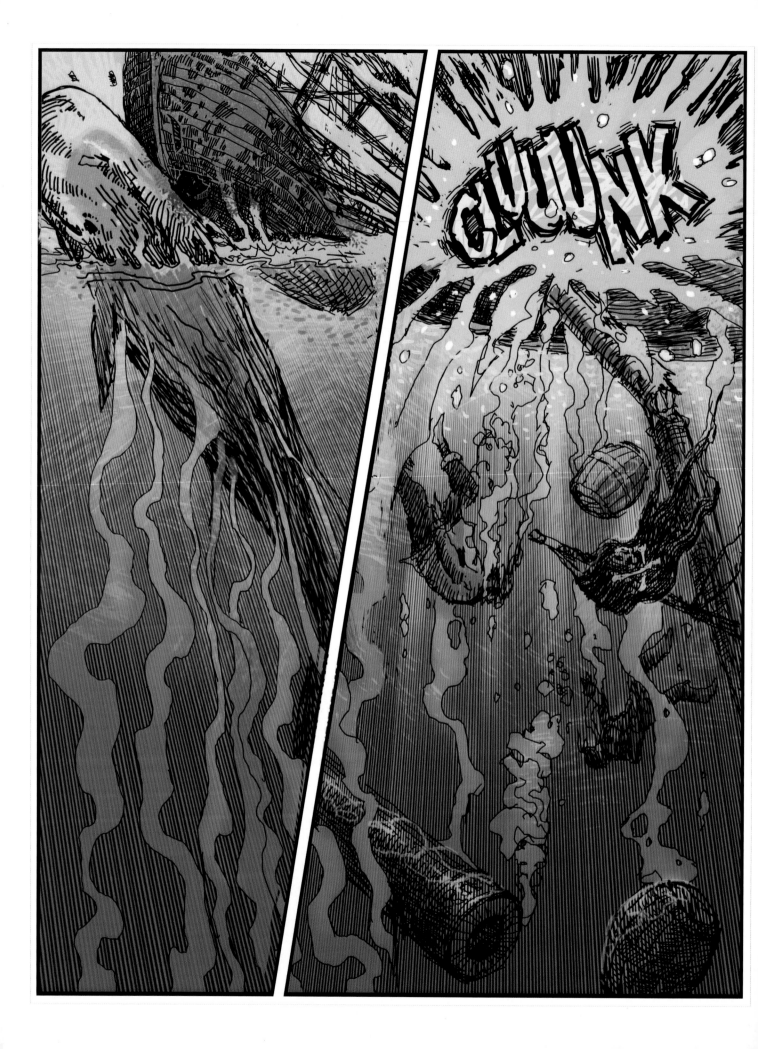

I *SAY*, THERE'S *PIPPA* AND *DAPH*. JUST IN *TIME* FOR TEA.

WE'LL GIVE YOU A *TOW!*

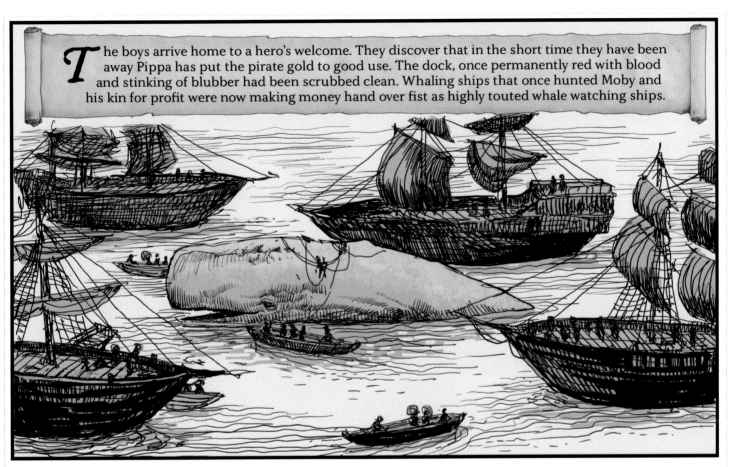

The boys arrive home to a hero's welcome. They discover that in the short time they have been away Pippa has put the pirate gold to good use. The dock, once permanently red with blood and stinking of blubber had been scrubbed clean. Whaling ships that once hunted Moby and his kin for profit were now making money hand over fist as highly touted whale watching ships.

"World's first selfie"

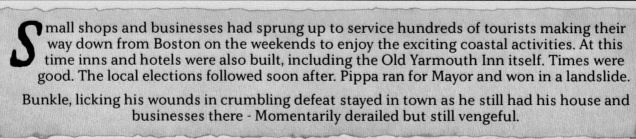

Small shops and businesses had sprung up to service hundreds of tourists making their way down from Boston on the weekends to enjoy the exciting coastal activities. At this time inns and hotels were also built, including the Old Yarmouth Inn itself. Times were good. The local elections followed soon after. Pippa ran for Mayor and won in a landslide.

Bunkle, licking his wounds in crumbling defeat stayed in town as he still had his house and businesses there - Momentarily derailed but still vengeful.

OH *LOOK* IT MADE IT.

GET OUT OF MY *SIGHT* BEFORE YOU RUIN THE *RUGS*.

A *TOAST* TO MY TOTAL *FUCK-UP* OF A *BROTHER!*

AND BY THE *WAY*, I'VE HAD TO *PROSTRATE* MYSELF IN FRONT OF *PIMPLE* TO CONVINCE HIM THAT YOU WERE A BLAMELESS *PRISONER* IN THIS WHOLE MESS. COST ME A *FORTUNE*, TOO!

YOU'D HAVE BEEN *HUNG* AT *DAWN*, BROTHER FUCK-UP.

Despite all Bunkle's setbacks, he announces that the ball is to go ahead as planned the following weekend.

He sees it as an olive branch to the local townsfolk but as usual, he is secretly plotting away and invites Pimple and other military high ups from Boston to attend.

WELL MAJOR, DO WE *TRUST* THIS?

WE *DO*, CAPTAIN HORNSBY, BUT WE KEEP OUR *EYES* AND *EARS* PEELED. YOU CAN *NEVER* TRUST A *BUNKLE*.

The next weekend arrives and it's the day of the ball. Ex-Mayor Bunkle is pulling out all the stops to make it the society spectacle of the year and has spared no expense. He's convinced himself that his social standing will be repaired and invites everyone in Boston society. Pimple and his wife are guests of honor and will be surprising the brave Yarmouth militiamen with medals of honor for their part in the Battle of Quebec.

As the party is in full swing, ex-Mayor Bunkle sidles along next to Pippa. Bellamy is nearby eavesdropping.

The three plotters huddle in a corner of the room as people all around them begin to sit down and fall asleep. Some lie fast asleep on the dance floor. Pippa and William watch aghast as one lady snores loudly face down on a piece of cake. Even the music starts to tail off as the musicians slide off their chairs.

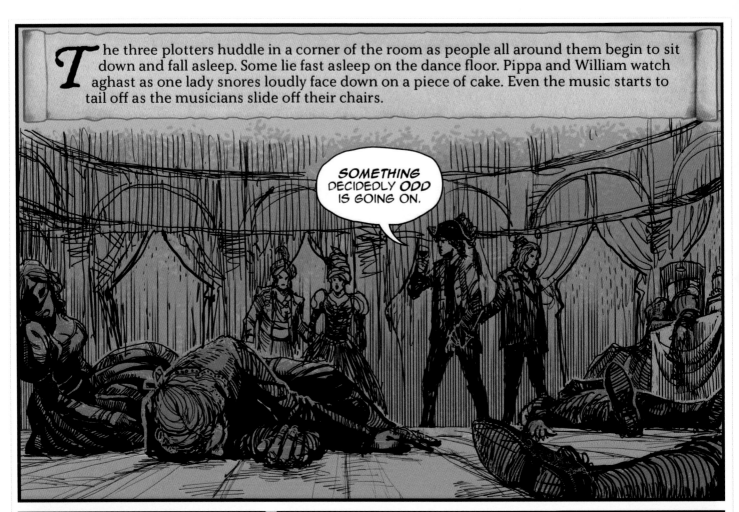

SOMETHING DECIDEDLY *ODD* IS GOING ON.

THIS *SMELLS* FUNNY. THAT'S *LAUDANUM.*

I THINK I *KNOW* WHO'S BEHIND THIS.

PIPPA, *WAIT!*

I DON'T KNOW *WHAT* YOU ARE *TALKING* ABOUT. LOOK WHAT'S *HAPPENED* TO MY WONDERFUL *PARTY!*

WHERE ARE THOSE *CONNIVING* CHILDREN OF YOURS? I *KNOW* THEY ARE AT THE *CENTER* OF THIS.

SURPRISE!

IT'S ME, *THE GREAT BELLAMY!*

GOOD RIDDANCE. THIS IS WAY HANDIER.

THAT'S A JOKE.

NOW THEN, MAYOR, I'D HATE TO RUIN THAT PRETTY FACE, BUT I NEED TO KNOW WHERE MY GOLD IS.

NOW YOU ARE GOING TO GET IT, BITCH! YOU SHOULD NEVER HAVE CROSSED ME!

IF YOU SCREAM, I'LL TAKE YOUR EYES.

3 PM, YOU SAY?

FWUMP!

OH MAYOR *PIPPA*, WELL DONE, YOU GOT THE *BASTARD*, AND THANKS TO *YOU* I'M *FREE* AT *LAST*.

YOU WOULD NEVER HURT A *LADY*, WOULD YOU? *GO GIRL POWER*, YAY!

GIRL POWER... YAY!

WHAP!

YOU'RE *NO* LADY. WELCOME TO *EQUALITY...* BITCH!

SORRY ABOUT THE *MESS*. WOULD YOU MIND *HELPING* ME CLEAN IT *UP*?

A little while later, the party resumes in full swing as everyone makes a full recovery. A footman bangs a gong and announces that everyone is to go to the ballroom for a big announcement. Everyone crowds around a podium as Pimple takes the stand.

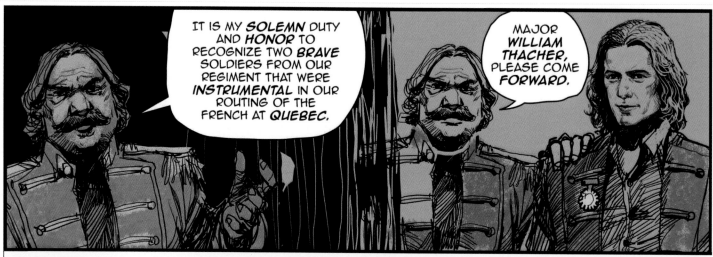

Pippa and William have an elaborate wedding at sea officiated by her beloved father.

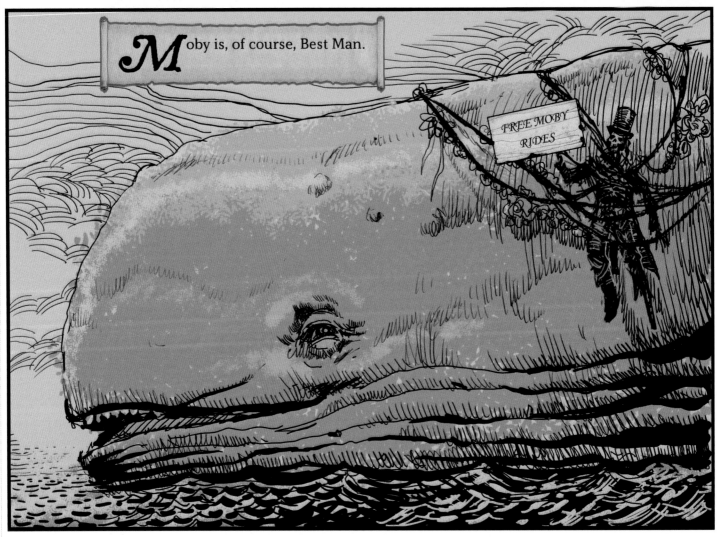

Moby is, of course, Best Man.

FREE MOBY RIDES

Madame Teteux proposes to her Amour who replies with a resounding *oui*--YES!

Many take part in Pippa's new self defense initiative.

A disgraced and totally soaked Felix and Felicity remove Moby's barnacles.

B unkle grapples with Pippa's healthy haute cuisine at the reception.

*P*ippa and the Major live to a ripe old age. They raised their children right here in this building which now is the Old Yarmouth Inn and their story will live on through the test of time as will their raucous spirits.

*T*he historical society wildly applaud and toast Sheila. The lights flicker as a distinct rumbling of horses' hooves is heard.

The End... for now!